Spilling the Beans on...

Robin Hood
and other robbers of the copse

Mile s
Kelly
PUBLISHING

First published in 2000 by Miles Kelly Publishing,
Bardfield Centre, Great Bardfield, Essex CM7 4SL

Printed in Italy

ISBN 1-902947-41-X

24681097531

Cover design and illustration: Inc
Layout design: Gardner Quainton
Art Direction: Clare Sleven

Spilling the Beans on...

Robin Hood
and other robbers of the copse

by Redvers Brandling

Illustrations   Mike Mosedale

About the Author

Redvers Brandling served in the RAF, before training as a teacher. He has worked in Singapore and Berlin and been a primary school headteacher and university tutor. Redvers has written over 50 books for children and teachers, and many articles and book reviews. His poems have appeared in various anthologies, and his short stories have been published in this country and abroad and been broadcast on BBC television and radio. He currently divides his time between writing, being a tutor on children's creative writing courses, listening to jazz and trying to play it on the piano.

CONTENTS

Chapter 1	Will the Real Robin Stand Up?	7
Chapter 2	Robin Rules the Roost	17
Chapter 3	How About a Fry Up?	29
Chapter 4	Why Were You an Outlaw Grandad?	42
Chapter 5	Sherwood Shockers	53
Chapter 6	A Tough Life	64
Chapter 7	Farewell Robin	80

CHAPTER I

Will the Real Robin Stand Up?

If there had been newspapers in Robin Hood's day, these might have been some of the headlines when he died. But not only were there no newspapers then, very few people could read or write. So the stories of Robin and his deeds were passed on by mouth. The mouths who told the stories were usually those belonging to travelling minstrels. These singers and entertainers were just like singers and entertainers today – they liked large audiences!

So, the way to get people to listen to them – and reward them more handsomely – was to make these songs and ballads as dramatic and exciting as possible. To do this they mixed a few facts with a lot of fiction and Robin's reputation grew and grew!

However, mixed in with these gripping tales told by the minstrels there were also some recorded facts. If we look at the two things together we can find evidence that Mr Hood was one of the longest living men ever.

1066 AND ALL THAT

We know that William the Conqueror invaded England in 1066 and that William the Red (William's son) was killed in the New Forest in 1100. These were the early Norman kings who sought to make the people of England obey their ways. They must have taken a long time because early stories of Robin Hood show him to be resisting Normans almost 100 years later. This was at the end of the 12th century.

Hey up lads – what about Yorkshire?

What about it indeed? In an Exchequer record called the *Pipe Roll* there is a section on Yorkshire which mentions a particular outlaw. Guess who? It was the man himself: *Robertus Hood – Fugitivus*. Now the date of this *Pipe Roll* was 1230. So if Robin had been fighting Normans more than thirty years earlier he must by now have been well into middle age.

Och aye – but what about North of the Border?

A man called Andrew of Wyntoun wrote a document in 1420. It was called *The Chronicle of Scotland*. In this report he mentions two outlaws who were very busy in Scotland in the year 1283. You will certainly be able to guess the name of one of them, and the other won't be much of a surprise either.

Their names were *Lytill Thon* and *Robyne Hude*.

So had Robin swapped forest green for a kilt in 1283? Was he really fighting the Normans in the 1190s? Was he that Yorkshire fugitive in 1230? If he was then you'll see why those imaginary newspaper headlines were sensational. Not many outlaws were still going strong when they were over 100 years old!

But just who *was* this mysterious man in green?

One of the most famous poems about him was called *A Gest of Robyn Hode*. The opening lines of this poem are:

Attend and listen gentlemen

that be of freeborn blood

I shall tell you of a good yeman,

His name was Robyn Hode.

But what was a 'yeman'? Well we know that this was just another way of saying 'yeoman', and a yeoman was a man of a village who farmed his own piece of land. So here we have Robin as a simple farmer and not a man of high rank.

"Rubbish!"

 Who said that? Lots of people if we believe some of the other stories of Robin. One tells us that he was a forester's son and that he was only 15 when he fought and killed 12 other foresters in a fierce battle.

"Rubbish!"

 Another story tells us that Robin's mother was a lady of high rank who fell in love with a servant.

"Rubbish!"

 Robin was the son of a squire. Now a squire was a gentleman next in rank to a knight, so this would make Robin far from being a simple farmer.

"Rubbish!"

Everybody knows that Robin was really the Earl of Huntingdon who had unfortunately lost his castle and all his lands. As a result he became an outlaw.

Phew! So who do we believe?

Whatever the differences in his background, however, all the poems and stories about Robin do agree about some things. He only robbed the rich to help the poor, they say. He loved the open-air life and was a great archer. He loved the summer and cared nothing for riches and castles when he had 10,000 acres of forest to roam and live in.

And now let's whizz right up to date. Your friendly computer will put you in touch with internet websites, which can give you lots of different ideas. Here's one example:

Despite Robin's 'legend' status there are many reasons to believe that Robin Hood could well have been a real historical figure.

The organization behind this website claims that there is evidence to show that there was a real outlaw in Nottingham at the time when Robin Hood was most famous.

So imagine we're there with Robin, Little John, Friar Tuck, Maid Marian, Alan a Dale, Will Scarlet, Much the Miller – and the villains – the Sheriff of Nottingham and King John.

What happens next?

But first unscramble your brain boxes and choose the correct answer from the following:

1. At the time, the stories of Robin Hood were told in:
   a. *The Medieval Beano*
   b. *The Sherwood Sentinel*
   c. Every newspaper in the country
   d. No newspaper at all

2. I'm the first Norman King of England and I'm called:
   a. King Norman I
   b. King William I
   c. King Kong
   d. King Richard I

3. How did the *Pipe Roll* describe Robin in 1230?
   a. Robin Hood – a tall man in bright green clothes
   b. Robertus Hood – Fugitivus
   c. Rogue Robin – the reckless robber
   d. The villain from the forest

4. Which document told us about Lytill Thon and Robyne Hood?
   a. *Our Island Story*
   b. *Magna Carta*
   c. *Hithtorical Thimes*
   d. *The Chronicle of Scotland*

5. Some people thought Robin was a nobleman. What was his title?

    a. Squire of Sherwood

    b. Earl of Huntingdon

    c. Supergreen

    d. Baron Rockingham

6. What was the name of the forest Robin lived in?

    a. Sherwood

    b. Windsor

    c. Old Reelie

    d. Bowmansgreen

7. What sort of bow did Robin use?

    a. Crossbow

    b. Strongbow

    c. Elbow

    d. Longbow

Answers: **1.** d **2.** b **3.** b **4.** d **5.** b **6.** a **7.** d

CHAPTER 2

Robin Rules the Roost!

"You want to be leader of the gang?"

"Are you the biggest, strongest, toughest, meanest guy around?"

Let's look again at Robin Hood. He must have been all of

these things – mustn't he? After all look at his reputation. First of all he was an outlaw. This meant that he had been ordered to attend court to face charges against him but hadn't turned up. He would have been given four more chances to appear and if he didn't he was then declared 'outside the law' – an 'outlaw'. If you were declared an outlaw any possessions you had were taken away and the money was given to the king.

Robin knew the only person who could pardon him was the king – but more of that later.

Meanwhile Robin was no ordinary outlaw. He became so famous – or infamous – that for about a hundred years after the time when he was most active, robbers and thieves were hardly ever called robbers and thieves. So, what were they called? You've guessed it – Robin Hoods. And even today outlaws in America are still often called 'hoods'.

You could just imagine a conversation in the years after Robin's day ...

So, Robin Hood had this fantastic reputation as a leader, but what were the qualities which made him one? Let's ask some more questions here.

 Was Robin the strongest of his group?

 He was a wonderful archer – but was he the best?

 Who was the best fighter with sword and buckler?

Before we go any further let's look for some answers to these questions.

One of the earliest stories of Robin took place when he was supposedly a young man of about 20. Out alone in the forest, he came to a narrow bridge. A stranger was already crossing it.

Did Robin politely stand back and wait until the stranger had reached the other side? No!

This was Sherwood Forest and Robin was used to having his own way around here. He too stepped onto the bridge ...

Now what happened next? Well, struggling and spluttering Robin scrambled to the bank and pulled himself out. Without wasting any time he pulled out his horn and blew for reinforcements. Within minutes of his summons various members of his band had arrived and surrounded the stranger.

Now, look at the facts so far:

Robin meets a stranger on a single track bridge.

Robin isn't pleased when the stranger chooses not to make way for him.

Robin threatens an unarmed man with a bow and arrow.

Shamed by his action Robin chooses to fight with only a staff.

Without too much effort Robin is swept aside.

As soon as he has lost Robin calls up his men to threaten the stranger.

So, are these the actions of a true leader?

No, you say, certainly not.

Ah – but what happened next?

Well, being surrounded, there wasn't much the stranger could do.

"What's your name?" demanded Robin.

"Sometimes I'm called Reynold Greenleaf and sometimes..."

"Well – go on."

"Sometimes they call me John Little."

At this Robin's men roared with laughter. What could be more ridiculous than to call a giant 'John Little?'

The laughter broke the ice. Soon there was a good feeling about the whole group – and then Robin showed one of his greatest qualities.

"Well John Little, now you've met us, will you join our group?"

There was a moment's pause and then the stranger spoke simply.

"I will," he said.

Amidst the back-slapping which followed a decision was made. From now on the giant would be known as 'Little John'!

But more importantly we have learned one of the qualities of Robin as a leader here. If he met a man who was stronger, a better fighter, and every bit as tough as himself, how did he solve the problem? Easy – he just asked his rival to join the gang, then he was on Robin's side. Shrewd man!

Now Robin's reputation as an archer was legendary. Again, tales of the group's deeds suggest he wasn't the very best man with a bow. One of the others, Gilbert of the White Hand, was at least his equal, so naturally he was quickly invited to be a member of the band!

TAKE AIM

But Robin was famous for his skill with the bow and arrow so let's pause and ask some questions about this.

What was the weapon like? Why was it so deadly? How good *was* good with it?

Now, keep this book in your right hand but stand up. Next, read the instructions in the following three sentences carefully, then put the book down and obey them!

1. Stand up as straight as you can. At full stretch.

2. Lift your hands and arms and stretch them out sideways as far as they will go.

3. Get a friend to measure this span – from the tip of one hand, right across your body to the tip of the other hand.

Right – sit down. Take a deep breath, relax. Why have we done this? Well, to find the correct length for an individual's longbow this measurement had to be taken. Then, the length of the longbow was cut to exactly this size.

OK. Now we know the length the bow needs to be, but how do we make it? The wood was usually taken from a yew tree. A groove was then cut in each end and the bowstring was attached to these grooves. The bowstring was generally made of hemp or flax. There was a grip in the middle of the bow.

FIRE!

Yeah – but what with? This of course was where the arrows came in. Like the bow they were very carefully made. This time the wood used was ash or birch. To add to their dangerous qualities the tip of each arrow was headed with a pointed

piece of iron. The flights at the back of the arrows were made of goose feathers.

Now we have a better idea of what a longbow was we need to know how good someone like Robin was at using it. For a start he could probably fire between 15 and 20 arrows a minute. This was a very rapid rate of fire. Secondly he would be very accurate at any range up to 100 metres and could certainly kill a man or beast at this range.

WHICH BOW?

In Robin's time there was lot of talk about whether the longbow or crossbow was best.

The crossbow was certainly more powerful but was very heavy to carry, sometimes needed a mechanical device to reload, and was more expensive to make. So – which would you rather have if you were an outlaw in the forest needing to move smartly?

SAY 'SAYONARA!' TO THE CROSSBOW!

Ouch!

Longbows... don't you just love 'em!

At last – a weapon that keeps pace with the modern archer!

Light, strong, fast, deadly ... and cheap

The Longbow will answer your needs ... and it won't leave a hole in your pocket!

CHAPTER 3

How About a Fry Up?

"Are you mad – or just bonkers, barmy and out of your mind?"

This is what your old granny might have said to you if you'd told her that you were going to spend a few days in Sherwood Forest in Robin Hood's time. Travelling then – anywhere – was dangerous and worrying and only a fool attempted it at night.

DON'T GO DOWN INTO THE WOODS TODAY

Sherwood Forest was first recorded in AD958, when it was called Sciryuda. It was established as a royal forest by William the Conqueror. In Robin's time the uncultivated part of the forest stretched for 50,000 acres and included 15 birch and oak woods which were separated by large areas of heath and grassland. Plenty of room to get mugged in!

The lonely traveller faced non-stop trouble. For a start there were Foresters, appointed to keep the laws of the forest. They suspected everyone they met of being a poacher. Their bosses, the Rangers, were always ready to demand a bribe off a traveller. If their victim didn't pay it he could be accused of almost anything. Then there were plenty of wild animals such as boars. All this is not even thinking about the violent thieves who roamed forests, and...aaaaahhhh!...medieval people were very superstitious and many feared monsters lurked in the dark and spooky corners hidden by trees.

So – who would be daft enough to be not only a traveller, but a regular traveller at this time? Well, strangely enough there was one group of people who chose to be just that.

FRYING TONIGHT

They were called Friars. These were religious men and the first
of them were followers of St. Francis of Assisi (you've all heard
of him – the patron saint of animals). Friars believed that the
monks of the time were wrong to cut themselves off and live
in monasteries. Friars acted on the words of Christ: "If thou
wilt be perfect, go and sell that thou hast and give to the poor,
and come and follow me."

So friars were to be found preaching, working with and helping the poor, and often because they had given up their own worldy goods ... begging.

All this talk about travellers, the dangers of the forest and friars has a point – as you will see.

News began to reach Robin of a friar who was in the area.

 He was no ordinary man.

 He was a good preacher, but he's a tough fighter as well.

 He didn't stand any nonsense from anybody at all.

These were the sorts of things Robin heard, and he wasn't pleased. Robin didn't like anybody else building up a big reputation in the forest. So he set out to look for this holy man. It didn't take long before...

"There he is!" cried Will Scarlet suddenly, as the band searched the forest. A figure lay dozing by some bushes near a wide, deep stream.

"Right, out of sight, I want some fun here," ordered Robin. The outlaws melted out of sight in the bushes and trees.

Robin approached the dozing figure. Then he couldn't help gasping in amazement as it stood up. It was the Friar sure enough. Dressed in a loose-fitting, belted robe with a large cross hanging round his neck, the holy man also carried a sword and buckler. On his head he wore a steel cap. But these were not the things which made Robin gasp.

"What a size!" the outlaw thought to himself.

The Friar was a very fat man indeed. Almost as thick as he was tall.

"With a figure like that no man could fight," thought Robin confidently. (A bit too confidently as we'll see!)

As Robin approached, the Friar watched cautiously. But he called a friendly greeting.

"*Pax vobiscum*, friend."

He was speaking Latin here. What he was saying was "Peace be with you." Robin mopped his brow and pretended to be very tired.

"I need some help from a good Christian like you," he said to the Friar. "I'm so tired. Could you carry me over that stream?"

Now if the Friar suspected a trick he was far too clever to show it. He nodded.

"Of course."

Taking Robin on his back, and showing surprising strength and agility, he carried the outlaw leader nimbly over the stream.

Robin was surprised at the ease with which he had got the Friar to do his bidding. He was even more surprised at what happened when they reached the other side.

"Now, you've had your fun with me," said the Friar as he put Robin down. "So just to show there are no hard feelings, you carry me back to the other side."

Before Robin could even catch his breath the fat, holy man had jumped on his back and was urging him on the return journey.

"I'll show him who'll have the last laugh," thought Robin angrily as they neared the bank again. "He needs a lesson."

Gasping and drenched he suddenly plunged the Friar into the water, and then immediately pulled out his sword.

"No more nonsense, carry me back to the other side, or else ..."

He waved his sword threateningly. Once again, to his amazement, the Friar gave in meekly, picked him up and set off once more across the stream.

"Huh, some fighter, this Friar," thought Robin dismissively.

That was his last thought for a while!

 Suddenly the Friar doubled up, and Robin went straight over his head into the stream. Drenched and furious he lunged to his feet. Instinctively he swept his bow from his back and fired an arrow at the smiling, soaked priest. He wasn't quick enough. The Friar flicked the arrow away with his buckler...

So ... back to the action ...

No sooner had the Friar swept away Robin's arrow than out came his sword.

For half an hour the two men fought. Sloshing and sliding in the mud and water their swords clanged through the still forest air. Fat he may have been but the Friar was inexhaustable. Robin dodged backwards, and finally dropped the point of his sword. He knew when enough was enough.

As the Friar paused too, Robin whipped out his horn and blew a rather tired blast. Within seconds his men in green were lining the river bank.

"So, you need some help, outlaw," smiled the Friar. He wasn't in the least bit frightened.

Now, as we've said before, Robin was a very shrewd man.

"Aye, we do that, Friar," he called, "We need a man like you to join us. To show us the error of our ways – and to look after us with that mighty sword." The rest of the outlaws cheered Robin's words.

The Friar calmly sheathed his sword. Looking at the tough men round him, he raised his hand.

"A blessing to you all." He called, and paused...and yes, I'll be pleased to join you."

Another great cheer broke out as the men helped Robin and the Friar out of the water. Once on land the Friar squeezed the water out of his cloak and began to tuck it above his knees. Watching him, one of the band called out.

"Seeing you do that, priest – and noting your figure – I reckon we must call you – Friar Tuck!"

More laughter.

Once again Robin had turned a difficult situation around to suit him. Another possible rival was now a member of his

band. This time, a holy man, admired and respected by all. A great catch!

But of course Robin had other qualities as well which appealed to the rough, tough outdoor men he led. He was lithe, fit and daring. Loyal himself, he inspired loyalty in others – and he was far from perfect! Supposedly a master of disguise, he could be described as daring – or foolhardy – depending on how you looked at it.

But more of that later, when we will also look at the man Robin considered his greatest enemy.

First let's continue our search for the truth. Are these statements TRUE or FALSE?

1. Little John was called this because he wore short trousers.

2. Longbows were called Christmas Crackers because you needed a holly tree to make them.

3. Crossbows were light and easy to use.

4. Robin Hood and Little John were good footballers.

5. Friars were very good at making chips.

6. Sciryuda was a sort of skin disease caused by not washing enough.

7. Rangers was the name of a Scottish football team that played in Sherwood Forest.

8. A buckler was used to keep your trousers up.

ANSWERS:

1. FALSE. No. They didn't wear underpants in those days –
   short pants were not a good idea.

2. FALSE. If you believe this then it is you who are crackers.
   Yew was the wood usually used for making a longbow.

3. FALSE. You must be joking.

4. There was evidence of football at the time, so the answer
   just might be MAYBE. TRUE!

5. If you said TRUE here, go to Macdonald's and volunteer to
   wash up for a week. Potatoes had not yet been discovered in
   England in Robin's time.

6. It's ok. You can put that soap down, the answer is NO.

7. FALSE. The sort of Ranger you might have met in
   Sherwood at this time would have been more likely to kick
   you than a ball.

8. You'd be better off with braces if you put TRUE here. The
   answer is FALSE.

CHAPTER 4

Why Were You an Outlaw Grandad?

If Robin had had any grandchildren this is a question they
might have asked him. But there is no simple answer to it. To
start thinking about some of the answers here are a few words
of poetry:

> We must be free or die, who speak
>
> the tongue that Shakespeare spake.

The poet who wrote this was called William Wordsworth (1770–1850), and both he, and Shakespeare, lived many years after Robin Hood. But what the poet says about being free had a lot to do with the life Robin chose.

What exactly does 'free' mean? Dictionaries have a lot to say about this word, but one definition is 'not bound by restrictions, not enslaved or in bondage.' That sounds very serious! But these words are an important clue to Robin's lifestyle. If for instance he was really born poor then he would have had no chance of freedom.

HARD LABOUR

Peasants at this time had to do exactly as the lord who ruled them ordered. They had to work for a number of days every week on his land – for nothing! The lord would give them small strips of land to farm for themselves as well. So, when they weren't working for him, they could grow food for their own families – but even then they had to give the lord some of the goods they produced on their own land! So free they weren't – but there were perks! If to you perks of a job means company car and pension, think again... a villager may have been be allowed to keep a sheaf of wheat as a bonus for harvesting his lord's crops and a shepherd's perk was to keep the use of twelve nights' dung at Christmas!

Peasants had neither the time nor the opportunity to travel anywhere. And if they tried to do something about this – WELL!

Let's say you are a villager and you decide to sneak away from your village to try and find a better way of life. If you are caught some rather unpleasant things might happen to you. You might be whipped, or have your tongue cut out, or your ears cut off. And, if you did escape, your family could starve to death without you there to help them. All very nasty!

So if Robin had started life as a poor man he would have needed courage to become an outlaw. But, perhaps anything might have been better than ordinary life.

We think Robin spent his summers in Sherwood Forest, and here again life was full of danger. Cutting a branch in a Royal Forest could result in a whipping. Using a dog for hunting could see the dog having its claws pulled out if you were caught. And – kill the king's deer... well just... goodbye!

To be an outlaw therefore Robin had to be daring, prepared to fight at all times, quick at escaping, clever with disguises. But you might ask, why did he rob wealthy churchmen in the forest? Sad to say, some of them deserved it.

WHAT ABOUT THOSE MONKS?

No matter how poor people were they had to give to the church. And some abbots and monks who lived in monasteries were not good men at all.

Listen to what Jocelin of Brakelond said in the early 1200s.

When Samson became abbot he spent a day of celebration with over 1000 dinner guests rejoicing greatly. As abbot he had several parks made for the abbey. He stocked them with wild animals and kept a huntsman and hounds. If an important guest was visiting, the abbot and his monks would sit in a clearing and watch the hunt.

Robin wouldn't have liked this!

Even if Robin had been born rich he still might have become an outlaw. Why?

To answer this question we first of all need to ask two more.

a) Who was Robin's greatest hero?
b) Who was Robin's greatest enemy?

The answers to these questions are:

a) King Richard I.

b) King John (and especially when he was Prince John).

Robin admired King Richard because he was a very similar man to himself. Handsome, brave and dashing, he was a famous soldier. But he was always off fighting crusades in other countries. This meant that John more or less ruled England in his absence.

SO WHAT ABOUT JOHN?

Here's what some people of the time might have said about him:

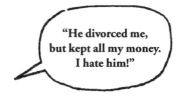

"He divorced me, but kept all my money. I hate him!"

His wife, Isabella:

Arthur, his cousin (or shall we say, the ghost of Arthur):

The Pope:

"I'd like to come back and haunt him. First he tried to have me blinded, then he murdered me."

"He wanted to make one of his useless friends Archbishop of Canterbury. I wasn't having that."

A baron:

"Money, money – that's all he thought about. He was always trying to get more money from us – *and* he wanted us to go and fight a hopeless war for him in France."

A peasant:

"Taxes, taxes, taxes. He'd try to make you pay taxes on anything, that man. And as for justice and fairness for the poor – forget it. There wasn't any."

So Robin was not alone in hating John – everybody did! If Robin was of noble birth then perhaps he became an outlaw because he a) he wanted to stop John's growing power whilst Richard was away, b) he might have had sums of money taken from him, c) he felt somebody should stand up for the common people or d) he couldn't stand being lawful if it was John's idea of law.

WHY WAS RICHARD CALLED 'THE LIONHEART'?

Let's imagine that there existed a newspaper which printed sensational stories at the time.

OUR MIGHTY MONARC
MAKES MINCEMEAT OF 'EM

CLEVER DICK

Richard the Lionheart is free and on his way home. For all of us loyal subjects who love him this can't be soon enough.

HEART-STOPPING!

Richard and two companions were on their way back from his latest crusade when they were unexpectedly attacked by a bunch of marauding Germans. They were thrown into the dungeons of their king.

Our king is free again… and how!

This king had a son called Ardour.

"Strongest man around," claimed the locals (they don't know our Rich).

Ardour (foolish lad!) told his dad that he wanted to teach this Englishman a lesson.

DEATH AT A BLOW

You are right, readers! Our mighty king killed his challenger with one blow. The German king was none too pleased.

"Take him to the lion's den," he screamed. "He'll pay for this."

So our Richard was taken to the king's private arena. Up went the grill and out leapt a lion – a very hungry lion!

King of men and king of beasts faced each other. But Rich got in first. Result: One dead lion.

"Let him go," yelled the German king. "Get him out of here. He's no ordinary man. He's got the heart of a lion, not a man".

So readers. Let's get ready for the big welcome back for our hero and our king – Richard the Lionheart!

Of course this is another legend – but you must admit it makes a good story!

The real reason for Richard's release is not quite so romantic. He was freed on the payment of a ransom of £100,000 – a gigantic sum of money in those days. And where did the money come from ? Of course – it had to be raised by the people of England.

As we have already said Richard spent far more time abroad than he did ruling England at home. It is not surprising therefore that he died abroad...

In March, 1199 Richard was besieging Chalus Castle in Limoges, a district of France. This was because the owner refused to surrender some treasure to him. During the fighting he was hit and wounded by an arrow. The wound was so serious that he died on April 6th, 1199. But that hasn't happened yet in our story.

CHAPTER 5

Sherwood Shockers!

See the
Madman
in his cage!

Kick the
Pig here

Place your
Bear Baiting
bets here!

What's this? Well we're about to learn how people had fun in Robin's day. Sad to say, so much of the 'fun' was very cruel.

Let's take bull and bear baiting for a start. First of all the bull or bear was held by a short chain and then hungry, savage dogs were set onto it. Terrible wounds were inflicted on the animals, and people bet on which dog they thought would survive the longest. Cock-fighting and dog-fighting were similar and equally popular.

You think this is bad? There is even worse to tell about. People who suffered from mental illness were very badly treated in these days. There was no medical help for them and they were dismissed as madmen fit only for sideshows. Sometimes they were put on show at country fairs so that visitors could stare at them.

Even those who might have known better behaved in a similar way. Matthew Paris, a writer of the 13th century tells us what happened to a monk:

The abbot was worried about his (the monk's) madness. He had him flogged until the blood flowed freely. After this ... the abbot had him chained and kept in solitary confinement until he died.

But, back to fun! Who is your favourite football team? You'll probably be quite surprised to hear that there are early reports of football in the 1200s! I doubt if it was very much like it is today ... although ... an early writer said it was ... "nothing but beastly fury and extreme violence". Hmmmmm.

The ball in those days was a pig's bladder stuffed with peas. So we might have heard the cry: "Kick the pig here."

ALL THE FUN OF THE FAIR

But what ordinary people looked forward to most of all in these times were the special days of the year. Fairs were held on such days and, as well as some of the cruel things already mentioned, there were also other exciting events. It was a noisy, bustling affair. Musicians, jugglers and acrobats would perform, pedlars brought goods from distant places and, if you could afford it, you might be able to buy cloth, leatherwork and weapons. For the ordinary and the poor there was the attraction of the food stalls selling hot pies, spicy wine and gingerbread. Everybody was out to have a good time, but all had to be aware of pickpockets and thieves. These fairs were well-organized too. Trading didn't start until the trumpet or the opening bell sounded. The weighing, measuring and quality of the goods were all inspected. Arguments were settled on the spot in a special booth. The 'court', which

settled problems, was called 'The Court of Dusty Feet'. this
name came about because some of the merchants had dusty
feet from travelling so far.

Out of all these special days one was looked forward to in
particular – May Day.

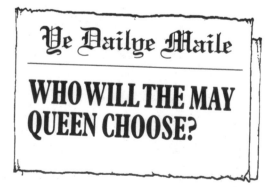

IT
COULD
BE YE.....

If there had been papers then these are the sort of things they might have said. May Day was May 1st and it meant that summer was returning. Girls washed their faces in early morning dew to look their prettiest. May (hawthorn) blossom was spread everywhere to bring good luck, and people cut down a special tree. This was usually an elm, ash, pine or birch. Then when it was decorated and stood upright once more it became the maypole. Everyone danced round it singing May rhymes and then ... the May Queen chose her Summer King!

So, let's get back to Robin, and why one particular May Day was so important to him. It started with a clash in the forest...

A MAY MAID

A crowd of people were following an ox-cart into Sherwood Forest. They were gaily dressed in green, yellow and white and some of them were playing drums and pipes. When they reached a clearing, a beautiful girl stepped forward and tied a ribbon round a tree trunk. The May Queen had chosen the Maypole.

But, before the tree could be chopped down the merry party was surrounded by Foresters who suddenly appeared from behind other trees.

"Stop!" bellowed their leader.

"No," replied the May Queen calmly. "It is our custom to choose our May tree every year."

"Not this year," snapped the Chief Forester. "The King's law says that no-one can trespass in the forest while the deer are carrying their young."

At this the Foresters began to drive the May Day group back, Staffs were out, blows were landed and then...

A second group of men burst into the clearing. Dressed in green they charged into the Foresters with drawn swords. Robin Hood and his outlaws had arrived just in time.

Soon the Foresters had been driven off and the outlaws helped to cut down the Maypole. Having loaded it onto the oxcart everyone headed back towards Nottingham.

"Surely you're not going into the town?" muttered Little John to Robin. "It's dangerous."

But Robin would have none of it, and when the group reached a square in front of a church in the town, the singing and dancing reached new heights. And then came the great moment ... the May Queen chose her Summer King. Well, I don't even need to tell you who she chose! And that's how Robin met Maid Marian.

Now Marian was a figure as mysterious as Robin himself and we don't know any real facts about her. But if you were to go through the oak woods to Edwinstone, near Nottingham, today, you would find a very old church. This is St. Mary'. It is mentioned in the Domesday Book and it is where, legend tells us, Robin and Marian were eventually married.

One of the traditions of May Day was that a swordsman cleared the way for the dancers. He was supposed to be getting rid of evil spirits and he often carried a cake with him – sometimes stuck on the end of his sword.

When the spirits were thought to have been driven off, the cake was broken up and shared amongst those celebrating.

Ye Recipe for May Buns

Ye ingredients:

100g butter, 100g caster sugar, 225g flour, pinch of salt, 1.5 teaspoonfuls baking powder, 1 egg, 2 tablespoonfuls milk.

Ye cooking technique:

1. Sieve flour and salt into a basin and rub in butter.
2. Add sugar and baking powder.
3. Add egg and milk and stir mixture until stiff. Divide up mixture into buns and place these well apart on a greased baking sheet.
4. Bake for about 15 minutes in oven 218°C/Gas mark 7 (ask an adult to do this).

Enjoy ye eats!

CHAPTER 6

A Tough Life

While Robin Hood was building up his band of men, meeting Maid Marian and having skirmishes with his enemies, ordinary people were carrying on with their lives. And it was tough!

If you were a peasant there was a good chance that you always felt hungry. For instance, how would you like to sit down to this feast every day:

Breakfast: Bread – coarse and dark, made from wheat or acorns.

Lunch: Er ... er ... bread, with perhaps a small piece of cheese. Once in a while a small piece of meat.

Supper: Soup – made from vegetables like beans and mushrooms and er ... er ... bread.

Drinks: Beer – home-made from barley. Goats' milk.

People who lived near the sea could have fish. Those inland reared pigs, sheep and goats but these were all very small compared to those we know today. Meat therefore was a real luxury. To hunt bigger animals was forbidden for ordinary people. Even fruit and vegetables were smaller than they are today. Of course there were no potatoes or tomatoes, the people of England had to wait centuries for those to arrive from the Americas. When times were really bad – after dreadful weather, sick animals, crop failures – then being hungry turned to famine and ... the poor had to eat horse meat, the bark of trees and even more unpleasant things. Many died of hunger.

HOW THE OTHER HALF LIVED

Not only was food meagre and often downright scarce but there was plenty of disease spread by things like dirty water and rats. Many children died before they were five and only the strongest and toughest adults reached 40 or more.

Life was tough!

If you'd lived in a village in Robin's time you would have certainly said this if you had known how 'the other half' lived. Nobles in their castles lived and ate very well. The castle stores were full of oats, wheat and barley, beef, pork, fish, salt and wine. The rich and powerful also ate venison, pheasant, partridge, hare and often finished a feast with a pudding! Meals in castles were served on trenchers on thick slices of brown bread. These soaked up the grease from the food, and at the end of the meals they were collected up and thrown to beggars outside the castle gates.

"After you, Claude."

Very important people might have said this. They weren't being polite – far from it. They were speaking to a taster, a man who had to taste all their food before they ate it – to check if it was poisoned!

So how well did Robin and his merry men eat?

Well ... *brede and wyne they had right ynough. And noubles of the dere. Swannes and fesanntes they had full gode. And foules of the ryuere.*

There you are – quite straighforward. They ate like this because ...

Robyn had in scherewod stod hodud and hathud and hosut and schod four and thuynti arows he bar in hits hondus.

Pardon? You can say that again!

These passages come from *A Gest of Robin Hood* and they make another point – we wouldn't have understood much of what Robin and his men were saying, even if we'd been there! People spoke very differently at this time. To give you some more examples, *daeg* was day, *wice* was week and *monath* was month.

So to translate the above pieces. . . The first one says: *Bread and wine they had right enough and entrails of the deer, swans and pheasants they had full good, and fowls of the river.*

The second piece tells us that they had these things because: *Robin Hood in Sherwood stood hooded and hatted and hosed and shot forth four and twenty arrows he bore in his hands.*

In other words Robin and his band ate well because they broke the law and shot deer and other game in the royal forest every day.

But legend keeps reminding us that Robin was a good man – he was a good *outlawe, and dyde pore men moch god.* (Ten out of ten if you can translate this yourself!)

WHY WAS THE LANGUAGE SO DIFFICULT?

You might ask why language was so different at this time. You might even feel sorry for folks who lived then because they had been used to speaking Anglo Saxon, but the people in the

north used a lot of Danish words too. Then the Norman kings and barons arrived – speaking French. They also made sure some Latin was used in churches! So as time went on the common language was Anglo Saxon, with a bit of Danish...with a bit of French...with a bit of Latin...Phew!

A NARROW ESCAPE

One day in Sherwood Robin heard the distant tolling of a church bell and decided he wanted to go to church. This led to one of his narrowest escapes, as we shall hear.

Robin decided he wanted to go to church himself and not take any of his men with him. Passing through the narrow streets of Nottingham he came to the church, went in and knelt to pray.

Now any thought that he could pass unobserved was madness on Robin's part. Even before he'd entered the church the whispers had shot round.

"Pssst – look who it is."

"Fancy Robin coming into town by himself – what courage!"

"Foolishness more like, he's certain to be captured."

"Never – not our Robin."

But as Robin knelt praying a monk entered the building. This was a greedy and selfish man who had once been held up by the outlaws in Sherwood. He recognised Robin immediately, quickly left the church and hurried to see the sheriff.

"I must see the sheriff at once." He cried on reaching the castle.

When the sheriff heard the news he was overjoyed. A troop of soldiers was summoned and soon they had the church surrounded. When Robin realised he was trapped he tried to fight his way out of trouble, but it was no good, there were too many for him. He was captured and imprisoned in the dungeons of the castle.

So Robin is in chains – but just who had got him, and what about this castle?

The Sheriff of Nottingham was the outlaw's greatest local enemy. But facts tell us that there wasn't a real Sheriff of Nottingham until this title was created in 1449 – long after Robin's heyday. There was however a Sheriff of

Nottinghamshire, who was the king's representative and had to enforce the law and gather taxes. Many of the sheriffs of the time were cruel, corrupt men, hated by everyone.

And what about the great castle at Nottingham in about 1200? Well imagine that there were estate agents at the time. If there had been this is how they might have advertised this fortress:

NOTTINGHAM CASTLE

KEEP THEM OUT!
YOU'RE SAFE INSIDE!

Secure fortress built in 1160s.
Protected by deep moat. Entry via
wooden drawbridge to gatehouse.
Good stone walls.

Inside – every luxury and convenience! Feed
hundreds in the Great Hall. Visit the chapel, stores,
kitchens, barracks, stables, bedrooms, spinning
rooms.

Stop press special!
Brand new hole-in-wall lavatories installed!

Feel safe! Permanent staff includes foot-soldiers
armed with bows, pikes and staves.

Be entertained! Jugglers, acrobats, jesters and
minstrels entertain regularly in the Great Hall.

Finest meals. Two hot meals a day from a team of
expert cooks.

No trouble! Dark, damp dungeons. Chains
available. When troublemakers go to our dungeons –
THEY STAY THERE!

And there in those dungeons Robin was chained. News reached the outlaws of their leader's capture, but also some other useful information.

"'T'was the monk who betrayed him. And for his reward he is to go to London to tell the king Robin Hood is captured."

At once the outlaws prepared. To get to London the monk and his servant must head south – and they'd be waiting for them. The ambush went as planned. Little John and Much the Miller's son took the messengers' places and, in disguise, went to London. There they gave the king the letter telling of Robin's capture. In return they got the Royal Seal for their leader's execution. They hurried back to Nottingham with this and made their way to the castle. Now it was more tricky!

"What's happened to the monk?" demanded the sheriff.

"Ah, the king was so pleased with him that he has made him Chief Abbot of Westminster. So we have brought the Royal Seal for him." Nobody recognised Little John and Much in their disguises and the sheriff was delighted to receive the seal.

There was feasting and drinking and the two outlaws were given beds for the night.

When everyone else was asleep John and Much crept down to the dungeons. The jailer was roused at sword-point and handed over the keys. Releasing a grateful Robin the three then climbed down the castle walls and made their escape. By dawn they were safe and sound back in Sherwood.

QUICK QUIZ

Can you pick the correct answer to each of the
following questions?

1. What was the main drink of villagers in Robin's time?
   a. Coffee
   b. Ovaltine
   c. Beer

2. Which poor people could eat fish?
   a. Those who had a fish and chip shop
   b. Those who lived near the sea
   c. Those with blue eyes

3. What was a taster used for?

   a. To see if the food was sweet enough
   b. To see if the food was poisoned
   c. To see if the food was too hot to eat

4. What was *monath* the old word for?
   a. Monarch
   b. Monday
   c. Month

5. Who did a sheriff work for?
   a. The king
   b. Cowboys living in England
   c. Ladies of the time

6. Which of the following might you have seen in the Great Hall of Nottingham Castle?

   a. Early television sets
   b. Jugglers
   c. A primitive CD player

Answers:

1. c. Beer

2. b. Those who lived near the sea

3. b. To see if the food was poisoned

4. c. Month

5. a. The king

6. b. Jugglers

Finally, something for you to think about. Which of the following jobs would you have liked least, and why?

a. Taster to a very important, but very unpopular person.

b. Castle lavatory cleaner.

c. Ditch and moat repairer.

CHAPTER 7

Farewell Robin?

The legends of Robin Hood tell us that despite being an outlaw
he was always fiercely loyal to King Richard. Because of this
Robin felt that he could be given a royal pardon if only he
could meet the king. Now, as we've seen, Richard I was
practically never in England during his reign ... and yet ...

"How do I find this Robin Hood?"

King Richard addressed the question to an old man who knew every trail and track of Sherwood. The old man looked at Richard and his knights.

"This is what you must do, my lord," he said. It was some time later that one of the outlaw band's lookouts saw six monks riding through the forest. Ahead of them rode an abbot. Quickly the message flashed back to Robin and, as the little party came into a clearing, they were stopped by the outlaw band.

"Halt, Sir Abbot," called Robin. "Your churches are rich in land and gold, what can you give us?"

This was how Robin challenged all travellers such as this.

So the abbot handed over money and the travellers were asked to eat with the outlaws. An archery competition followed and when Robin missed with a shot he insisted the abbot hit him for his inaccuracy. When the abbot did this his cowl fell off and all saw – that it was King Richard!

The outlaws all fell to their knees, vowed their loyalty, and were pardoned by the king.

"But you must give up being outlaws," ordered the King, "and come and serve me at my court."

So ...

Was this the end of the merry men?

What happened next?

And of course the answer is, as usual ... nobody really knows, but...

The Gest of Robin Hood says that Robin could only stand being away from Sherwood for a year, and so he returned to his old life there. Some say that this was for as long as 22 more years.

What was the end then? Well, before we get to that we need to discuss some medical matters.

MARVELLOUS MEDICINE

Now, are you feeling all right? No headaches, tummy aches, tooth aches? Good. It is always good to feel well. But if you didn't in Robin's time...oh dear oh dear oh dear!

People in medieval times were terrified of becoming ill – and they had every reason to be. For a start they didn't realise what caused their illnesses – the unclean food, dirty water, insufficient washing of bodies and clothes – all of which allowed germs to spread. Cleanliness was of no importance at all. People were often infested with fleas and other nasty creepy-crawlies which found their way into very private parts of the body. There was even a certain type of worm which found its way inside the body and then popped out through a convenient hole – such as the corner of the eye! One way to get rid of these pests was to have a good wash – but it never occurred to anyone! On top of all this many people were often weakened by not having enough to eat.

When you became ill in these times your chances of getting better were very much a case of luck. One reason for this was that there were very few doctors, and these concerned themselves mainly with rich people who could pay them. Ordinary people consulted 'wise women.' Usually each village

had a wise woman, someone who knew which mixtures of herbs would help pain and illness. Surprisingly enough some of these cures worked.

It was also thought that illness was a punishment from God, so praying was considered important in trying to cure the sick. If you had something wrong with you which needed an operation to put it right then you were in real trouble!

There were no anaesthetics to help with operations so you felt every bit of pain. There were no antiseptics so you could easily catch infection from the surgeon's instruments. And,

worst of all you might think, doctors often thought they were too important to perform operations so the job was left to people who combined this with being a barber!

Here is what somebody wrote at the time:

Surgeons should cheer up their patients by telling them to be brave when they are in great pain. It is useful if they can tell good jokes to make their patients laugh.

Now let's think about something else horrible – toothache!
If you were really brave, or desperate, you could have the
painful tooth pulled out. No anesthetic of course, and
sometimes this was done in a tent at the local fair. While you
were having your tooth removed a drummer played long and
loud – to drown the screams of pain!

OK, so you're not brave enough to have this dental
treatment – what else can you try to stop the toothache? Well,
how about the following:

Take a candle of mutton fat and burn it as close as possible
to the tooth. Hold a bucket of cold water underneath. The heat

of the candle will make the worms that are gnawing the tooth want to escape, and they fall into the water.

Ugh – I know, I know – you'll never complain about going to the dentist again!

Now you might ask, what has all this to do with Robin? Well, quite a lot, as you will see.

Old age was catching up with our outlaw hero. He didn't feel well and decided he needed some medical treatment. Now we haven't mentioned one of the most highly thought of cures of the time. This was bleeding the patient. It was thought that illness was often due to bad blood. The patient was therefore cut and allowed to bleed so that the bad blood could escape from the body.

Robin felt that this was what he needed. So he and Little John set off for Kirklees Priory where his aunt's daughter was the Lady Prioress. But what Robin didn't know was that this Prioress was a great friend of one of his worst enemies – Sir Roger of Doncaster.

So, when the Lady Prioress cut the veins in Robin's arm, it was not to cure him, but to kill him. And so we have the sad legend of Robin's death. Weak and dying from loss of blood, he called the faithful Little John to him.

"Give me my bow," gasped Robin. "I will fire a last arrow. Where it falls – bury me there."

Little John did this and Robin was buried where his last arrow fell. But the mystery remains. Later his grave was opened – and there was nothing and no-one in it.

Property of R. Hood.

THE LEGEND LIVES ON

As we have said before, there is no real factual evidence to show when or if Robin ever lived. The same applies to almost everybody else in his story, apart from the kings, Richard and John.

And yet, can there be a more famous man in English history? His name lives on throughout the world as well as in England. He has been the subject of films, TV programmes and popular songs. When a part of modern rural Nottinghamshire was to be turned into a housing estate protest posters appeared. They were signed by ... Robin Hood. In Cumberland there is a place called Robin Hood Butts; in Hampshire somewhere called Robin Hood's Barrow. Between them there are 85 other places with the name 'Robin Hood' in them. Probably, as you read this, there have become more. Robin lives on...

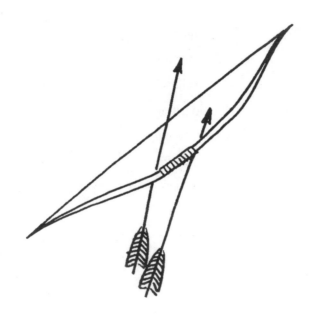

And finally, if you want to find out more about Robin and his times try and visit Sherwood Forest Country Park and the Robin Hood collection at Nottingham Central Library, Angel Row, Nottingham NG1 6HP.

titles in the series

Spilling the Beans on Julius Caesar

Spilling the Beans on Einstein

Spilling the Beans on Tutankhamen

Spilling the Beans on Shakespeare

Spilling the Beans on Robin Hood

Spilling the Beans on Napoleon